BRAVE
A COLORING BOOK FOR GIRLS THAT CAN

AUTUMN
PUBLISHING

AUTUMN
PUBLISHING

Illustrated by Anne Passchier

Designed by Charlie Wood-Penn
Edited by Hannah Cather

Copyright © 2021 Igloo Books Ltd

Published in 2021
First published in the UK by Autumn Publishing
An imprint of Igloo Books Ltd
Cottage Farm, NN6 0BJ, UK
Owned by Bonnier Books
Sveavägen 56, Stockholm, Sweden

Manufactured in China. 0621 001
10 9 8 7 6 5 4 3 2 1

Library of Congress Cataloging-in-Publication
Data is available upon request.

ISBN 978-1-80108-740-7
autumnpublishing.co.uk
bonnierbooks.co.uk

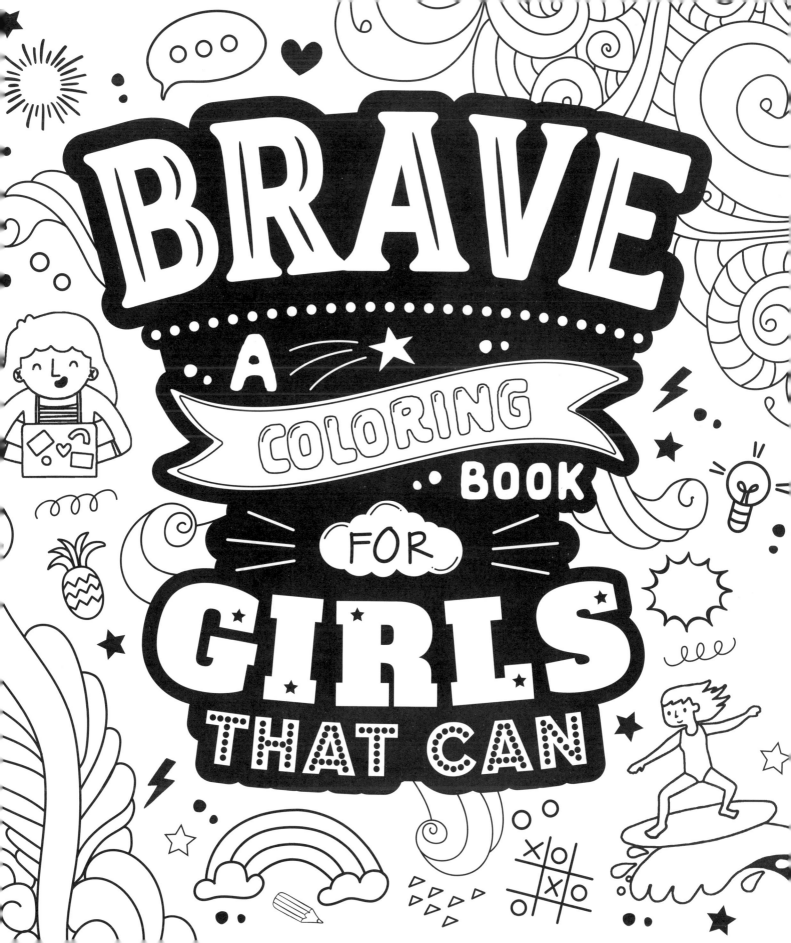

SHE BELIEVED SHE COULD,

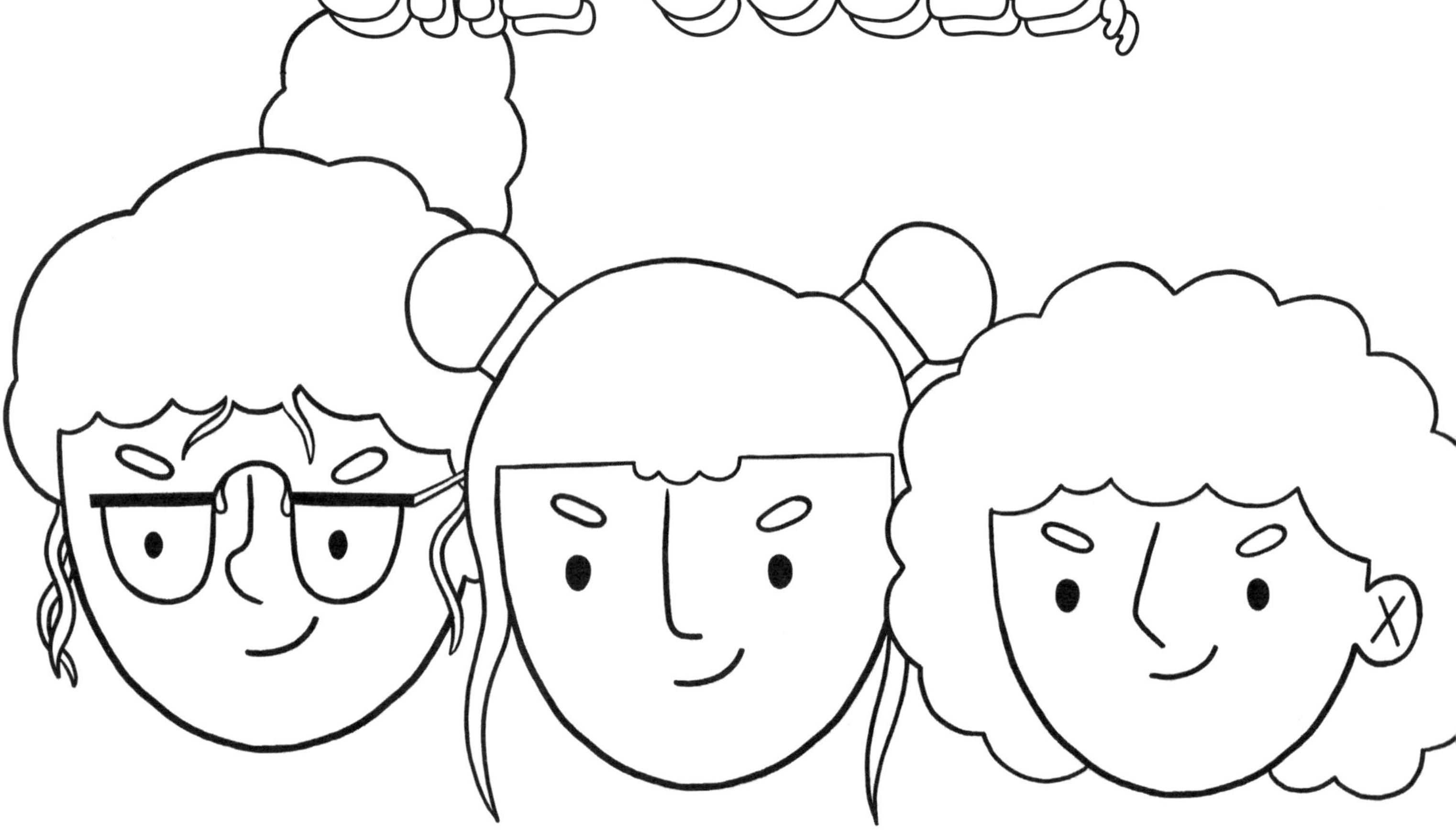

SO SHE DID.

A girl should be two things:

WHO AND WHAT SHE WANTS.

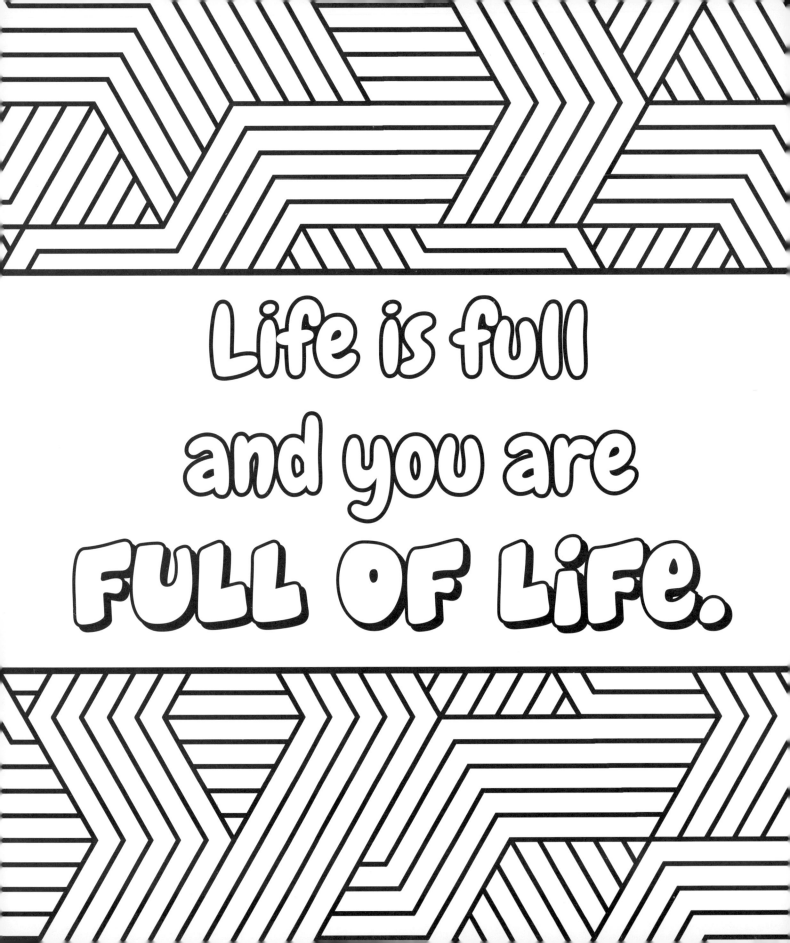

Life is full
and you are
FULL OF LiFe.

YOU ARE MAGIC, RADIANT, AND POWERFUL.

YOU MATTER.

WHAT ARE GIRLS MADE OF?

DETERMINATION.

Heart.

Power.

Empowered girls empower girls.

She is sunshine, mixed with a little hurricane.

DO MORE OF WHAT MAKES YOU HAPPY.

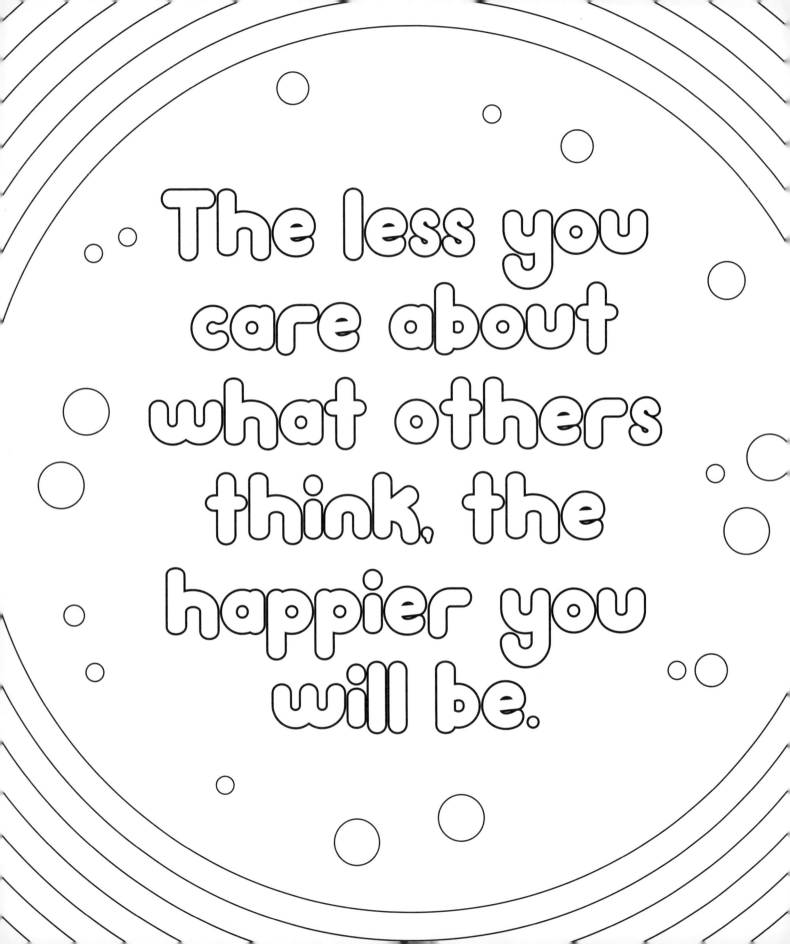
The less you care about what others think, the happier you will be.

Fight for the things you care about.

NOTE TO SELF:
YOU ARE
ENOUGH.

Behind every girl is... HERSELF.

She's got that whole
CHANGE-THE-WORLD
kind of vibe.

NEVER STOP LEARNING. LEARN SOMETHING NEW EVERY DAY.

Surround yourself with positive people.

I'm pretty... INCREDIBLE.

Girls with dreams
become women
with vision.

Beautiful days BEGIN WITH beautiful mindsets.

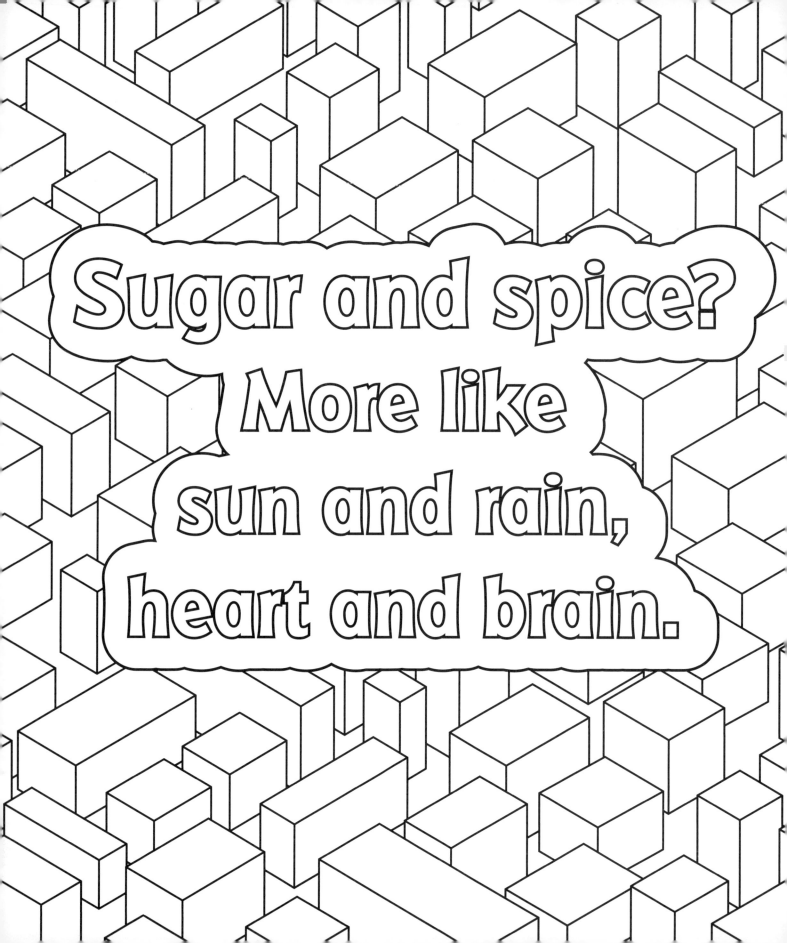

WILD and FREE and HAPPY.

Fierce soul.
BRAVE HEART.
Strong mind.

The world is yours
for the taking.

Get out there!